Poetry of the Heart:
A Journey through Emotions

Maha Griffin

DEDICATION

This book is dedicated to my children: I want to give you happiness and love. I have become inspired by your creative minds and your ability to image through play. Your unconditional love and innocents has brought happiness to my life.

Poetry of the Heart:
A Journey through Emotions

CONTENTS

ACKNOWLEDGMENTS

I would first like to acknowledge the readers of this book. Thank you for reading these poems. I hope they heal, inspire, enlighten, and provide passion for your minds and spirits.

I also want to acknowledge my close friends for the feedback they gave me for some of my early work, and my husband, Marlon Griffin, for his motivation and support during the process of writing this book.

To my brothers, Fahd, Sultan, and Yusuf, who did their part with the necessary details of the book.

I would like to acknowledge my mother, Nancy Al-Hibshi, for being a strong woman and always enjoying my poetry.

To all the people who have had an influence in my life, you know who you are.

Lastly, I would like to acknowledge God for guiding me along this journey of writing what I see and feel.

<u>Upbringing</u>

Trying to fit in the box of society

and allowing myself to be mold in their perception.

The fear of being me

destroys my innovation.

With no solid ground to stand on

and no real culture to claim.

No steady path to follow along

and a fake family last name.

I grew up lost in confusion

with no father to look up to…

and a stepfather lost to drug addiction

while going to a school that's always new.

Regret had always been in my heart;

the thought of what could have been.

Wishing my parents never were apart;

wishing they made a better decision.

My mother, too busy working to raise me;

she struggled to provide.

My father neglected his family;

I never got to ask him why.

So along the path of destruction I went;

got pregnant at nineteen.

This world had nowhere for me to fit.

I never pursued my dream.

Too scared that it wouldn't come true.

Feared that I would be successful

at what I put my mind to.

Gave up on goals and began to settle.

No longer will I let my past set my course;

I've broken the chains of regret.

And no longer make choices that cause remorse,

for my thoughts create the effect

of the life I choose to live.

The life I choose to have now

and the things I once did.

My society is what I allow.

I can create my own steady path

with my ambition.

I can turn a cry into a laugh

with a self-created perception.

<u>Late</u>

It's never too late

to write your heart.

It's never too late

to open your soul.

It's never too late

to try to start.

It's never too late

to let it go.

It's never too late

for something new.

It's never too late

to follow a dream.

It's never too late

to make it come true.

It's never too late

to cross a stream.

<u>Rain</u>

The wet raindrops

hit my window on the top

and slide down to the bottom.

As I glance outside the window,

I look through the glass.

My eyes search for the sun,

but the gray clouds in the sky

cover the light.

My right hand holds my head up

as my elbow rests on the window sill.

My elbow aches with the weight of my head.

My eyes are weak from moving too fast.

My brain is exhausted from thinking about life.

<u>Mom</u>

Salute to a warrior of love.

The one with a protective hug.

The soldier who fought for me to live.

The person who cared about her kid.

I give honor to you for all you do

and all the hardship you went through.

You battled the hardest fight.

You took care of me, raised me right.

You put your needs aside to meet my own.

And what's amazing is you did it alone.

I wish you luck on your endeavor,

and will honor you forever.

Because of you, I am who I am today.

Thank you for paving the way.

My gratitude will forever remain.

My appreciation will never fade.

Not only do you work hard for your children,

you also unconditionally loved them.

You are the warrior mother,

and there is no other.

Lost

Pain cut through my veins like a knife.

Why did God take you out of my life!

It hurts to think that you are gone.

Without you around it seems wrong.

I lost you,

yet I will never forget

all the beautiful memories I've kept.

The love you've shown.

The way you would smile.

I'll admit, I'm still in denial.

Your work on earth is valued and cherished.

The thought of you will never perish.

It's comforting to know you're in a better place.

Just remember, you'll never be replaced.

As the warm, salty tears slowly slide on my cheek,

I try to breathe in strength, yet feel weak.

Without you, life is not the same.

Guess I should adjust to this change.

<u>Helpless</u>

A cold heart

made by the streets of the city.

Torn into pieces by sights so awful

it cannot be comprehended

by simple minds that do daily tasks

in a simple, pleasant world.

The far end of the stick is the first to feel

the motion of the street.

Hear the cries of pain;

become numb to the helpless voices of despair.

Only walls can close in on the suffering,

yet walls are not thick enough for protection

from the bullets that pierce so fast

into the soul of a helpless warrior.

Where is your strength, I wonder?

How can you be strong when your limits are pushed to the ground

and you no longer can stand up

for what you once believed in?

Pain is what covers your eyes;

like shades of visions that never disappear.

In the remorse of the choices made,

how can you feel the same

in that old simple town you left behind?

Now nothing is seen the same,

for it will remain in your heart:

the pain of the helpless souls

that are lost in the sand

and will never return.

You wonder what is it all for,

if nothing makes any sense.

Yet you feel that it is not the way you thought it would be.

Since you continue to be helpless with no direction to follow

and no strength to walk,

then you leave it in God's hands to be strong for you

and have faith that he is love.

<u>Existence</u>

Sorrow is covering my eyes.

Change comes with no surprise.

The past is a sad memory.

The future seems so lonely.

If I struggle long will I grow?

Now I feel I am only getting old.

It seems my destiny is misery.

For what comes is always empty.

I'm passing this world with no hope.

My faith became a broken rope.

My imagination becomes my reality,

because what is real is too painful to see.

Obstacles become hard to overcome,

and enemies beat me like a drum.

I continue to try and try,

yet still get pushed aside.

They restrain my strength with a chain,

Yet my existence will remain.

<u>Love Spell</u>

My desire for him is lust.

Flames burning inside with each thrust.

My body falls limber from his every touch.

The very essence of his presence makes me sink;

I sink deep into a love spell.

His warm body sinking into my skin

makes me want to commit a sin.

Falling deeper and deeper as I let him in.

His eyes touch my soul deep as I sink;

I sink deep into a love spell.

Every day I want him more and more.

His soul, body, and mind I want to explore.

The sound of his voice makes my heart drop to the floor.

The more time we spend I fall deep and

sink deep into a love spell.

He knows he has me in every way.

He can control my mood each day.

Now things start to go insane.

I depend on him to pull me up as I

sink deep into a love spell.

The curse is on me, and now I'm weak.

My heart can get broken as I sink.

Will I drown

or will I breathe

deep into a love spell.

Cheated

My heart was trusting of our love.

We fitted like a hand and glove.

Attraction, happiness, and amazement.

Phone calls, text messages, and time spent.

We could not get enough of each other.

You were my perfect lover.

Then you let her come in;

you let a seduction win.

Went to her without me in your head.

Stopped loving me as you lay in her bed.

You wanted another woman then

even when we were happy, and

now you say sorry for what you did

and can't explain why it happened.

Gave an excuse to explain why

you forgot your love was mine.

Love didn't stop you from going to her home.

Love didn't stop you from telling her no.

Your love must be weak 'cause mine is strong.

My love keeps me from doing wrong.

You destroyed my innocent love I had.

You created this attitude that's always mad.

My trust is killed, and now you want to move on!

Get over it and move on!

Grow up and move on!

I'm immature, just move on!

I'll let go when I'm gone.

I'll let go when you hurt, too,

and know how it feels to lose.

Word Effect

When he would step in

He used words as a weapon,

Did I create this aggression?

I'm his target used at his discretion,

whether that may be love or deception;

it depends on what mood he is in.

How can this person's words have such an impact on me?

Why is the one I love my number one enemy?

I'm crying, hurting every day with pain, but I don't leave,

because who he truly is, I don't want to believe.

Is this what love is, or what I deserve,

hurting each other with a word?

It wasn't always like this;

in the beginning it was happiness and pure bliss,

now each other, we seldom miss.

It was butterflies in my stomach, nonstop kissing,

lovemaking, and cuddling,

admiration, inspiration, respect—now it's struggling.

Now I don't allow our eyes to meet.

I'd rather ignore you than get shot by words when you speak.

I once was a strong, secure woman, now I'm weak.

<u>Broken Heart</u>

You'll never know how bad it hurts.

You just keep making it worse.

How long did you think I would take it?

How long should I fake it?

This isn't love, it's not right.

I didn't see this becoming my fight.

If you're so unhappy then leave,

because I'm not afraid to breathe.

Without you, I feel free,

and I can be me.

When you are around, I'm pushed aside.

I'm belittled and criticized.

You have no interest in my dreams;

what I like and what makes me happy.

You only want things your way,

and hush me when I have something to say.

You tricked me; I did not know

that this is the real you, because long ago

there was a spark in you, a light.

Being with you felt right.

I used to be excited to see your face.

Now you search for a person to replace.

What we had in the beginning was real.

Now it's like I can't even want or feel.

Nothing will ever be the same.

The love we had is drained.

You broke me to the point of no return.

Is this what I deserve?

Wish I could go back in time

and erase the day I called you mine.

A Love Roller Coaster

She sits, lonely.

She has nobody.

Misery is her company.

How could he be so damn deceiving?

The makeup can't hide

the tears she's cried.

She laughs away her pride.

Her image broke the day he lied.

She sits, lonely.

She would erase the day they met

on the corner of market,

at the café drinking her chocolate.

He became her only threat.

She sits, lonely.

Being with him was her sacrifice.

She gave up her social life

and decided to become his wife.

His dishonesty pierced her heart like a knife.

She sits, lonely.

Years invested and she was unaware

of his secret love affair.

She tried looking sexy and fixed her nails and hair.

He didn't notice and continued to not care.

She sits, lonely.

He sits, lonely.

He has nobody.

Misery is his company.

How could she be so damn deceiving?

A beautiful queen;

he fell in love at a club scene.

Couldn't believe she was a single lady.

Then everything about her became shady.

He sits, lonely.

He gave her the world without a question.

Just wanted her love and affection.

Told her to be honest and never become a deception.

He found out she was causing another man's erection.

He sits, lonely.

Took her around his friends and family.

Invited her to share a mutual dream.

Wanted to create an empire with her on his team.

Didn't know she was taking his money.

He sits, lonely.

His pride wouldn't admit his hurt.

He went out to date and flirt.

Behind her back he did his dirt.

She tainted his trust, so he chased another skirt.

He sits, lonely.

They sit, lonely.

They have nobody.

Misery is their company.

How could love be so damn deceiving?

Baby Mom

Beautiful young lady

fell in love with a cat named Johnny.

Thought sex was love and made a baby,

now she's a single lady.

Trying to complete her college degree,

getting judged by peers and faculty

as she is always late to the university

because the sitter couldn't make it until three.

While her friends enjoy the beach

she's home feeding her son a peach,

trying to remember what the professor would teach.

Studying at 2:00 a.m. for her public speech.

While her peers enjoy the club scene,

she's working part time to make ends meet.

Going home and keeping the house clean.

Making sure the baby has enough to eat.

Met a guy in her school.

Promised he would take care of her and make her his boo.

Now she was looked at as a fool;

became a single mother of two.

Her kids became her motivation.

She finished school with determination.

She never quit in any situation

and became a strong single mother of this nation.

Rise up single mom, don't quit.

You are worth it.

Don't torment your wit.

Embrace the unique strength you emit.

<u>Blind Love</u>

A person will say they love you,

yet ignore you when they look your way,

or glance the other direction

when you are trying to get their attention.

They say they love you

and pay no mind

to what you have inside,

yet they want your body to feel.

For those moments you think love is real.

You become less and less important to them,

and they shut you out until they are ready again.

You think you have a good one

until you see the wrong, so why do you keep holding on?

Is it worth the pain you feel when you stick around

to just keep allowing someone to beat you down?

Fooled

Was it love?

I was robbed of my innocent affection,

he took my very own perfection

and made me become something I am not.

I thought he was the one.

A man with goals and words shot faster than a gun.

He fooled me.

I thought he would always be gentle;

I didn't know his car was a rental.

He wasn't real.

He made me think I found a blessing,

gave me kisses while I was resting

and spent time with me.

I trusted no other woman had his attention,

then I found out the truth of my sexual infection

but he was sorry.

He cried and begged on his knees,

promising that he would always love me

yet I was continuously disrespected.

He promised he would change

and we would be engaged,

then it happened again.

Another woman took his attention;

though he kept begging for affection,

my heart was broken.

We built a love, how could I leave,

separating would only make me unhappy.

How would I find peace?

How do I stop arguing, thinking he would feel my pain;

hiding from others because I became ashamed.

This isn't me.

What happened to the woman I created;

now I've become the woman he hated.

The nagger.

He wants love and respect.

How can I give it if it's not given?

I became verbally abusive,

then he lost control,

and the gentle touch became a harsh blow.

I can feel the sting.

He said he was sorry

and would never do anything to hurt me.

I was trapped.

How do I get out of this hole?

How could he affect my soul?

No one should have that much control.

I'm taking back my dignity.

I'm taking back my individuality.

Give me my heart.

I'll decide when I will love.

I will determine once I have enough,

and I will be just fine.

<u>Bitter Woman</u>

She sits in her corner sad and confused,

not knowing what to do.

Her life has changed, and she's alone

handling the problems on her own.

She walks through the world with no direction,

running through a maze of deception.

How the hell did she get to this place,

she doesn't even recognize her face.

She tries to put on a mask,

but the fake emotions won't last.

She feels hate inside her heart,

he destroyed her from the start.

He made her weak, then fall in love.

She was hooked to him like a drug.

Then he turned on her and crushed her soul.

Now she has no joy to hold.

Misery is her best friend,

and the lies will never end.

<u>Closing the Door</u>

I bet you never thought this would happen.

Everything was perfect back then.

Now it's a nightmare that won't end.

When did we become so distant?

I don't know where the happy story went.

I thought our love was heaven sent.

I guess I was wrong about us.

Yes, it's true I lost trust.

Yes, my happiness turned to dust.

But look at things from my view.

Put yourself in my shoes.

I've asked for attention from day one.

All you ever did was run.

You laughed at me when I was falling.

You didn't answer when I was calling.

My heart broke when you left my side.

I guess you and I were a lie.

But all you see is a woman nagging.

You laugh while my heart is dragging.

How can I express who I am

if you never give me a chance to stand?

Internal Battle

Grew up with low self-esteem,

many men who wanted me

made me feel like a queen.

Found out they wanted my body

since they were lusting,

and I became someone they were using.

What happened to the Prince Charming,

the man specifically designed for my need?

Guess I didn't wait patiently.

Didn't know I was living

in misery

caused by choices I was making.

I looked at my life and wondered why

did I

create a world I despise?

And everyone says sorry,

can't help me,

but will continue praying.

Close friends became enemies;

anyone who gets near me

grows jealous and would flee.

How I longed for a real friend,

someone who was there through thick and thin,

kept thinking it would never happen.

Felt an emptiness in my life to my soul,

lost all control,

and had no room to grow.

Fought a battle that wasn't mine,

lost every time,

and kept searching for a sign.

Poor lost girl, they thought,

always in the club a lot,

finding happiness in places where it's not.

They never stepped into my shoes,

this isn't the life I choose,

and I continue to lose.

I gave up trying to fight

since doing it alone wasn't right,

I began to pray every night.

Guess praying changed my path,

went from a cry to a laugh,

so you can do the math.

Dream

I saw myself in a house

wearing an expensive blouse.

I saw myself wealthy with fancy cars.

Dreamt so big I could touch the stars.

I saw weekend vacations, exotic hotels in paradise.

What everyone's life should be like.

I saw friends and family all around.

Happiness is what I've found.

I opened my eyes and woke up to reality.

I stared at a one-bedroom apartment in Queens.

Had a thousand bills not paid on time,

and living a life in grime.

I stared at my distant family and friends

who wanted to mess up my plans.

I stared at struggle and pain,

so I closed my eyes to dream away

and hoped to wake up to a better world

where I could have everything I wanted and more.

Don't wake me up from this dream.

I refuse to face reality.

James 1:12

My trials,

the hardship in my life.

The loss, anger, frustration, and hopeless fight.

They say be strong during tough times,

or that these times are meant to make you strong.

During these unforeseen moments in trials,

thoughts of giving up become worthwhile.

Where do I get the strength to continue on?

Where is the motivation coming from

to hold on?

What drastically changes a frown to a smile?

What good do I get from this trial?

They say blessed are those who make it

through the hard times.

I think it's because of their powerful minds.

Although I've conquered these trying moments,

with what weapons did I use to fight the tests?

And how does it change who we are?

The person we've become from our scare?

My past turmoil motivated me to succeed.

Though this is not the case for everybody.

Wasted

The past became a blur.

A vision not welcomed.

A thought turned to painful feelings

because it was wasted.

Time, how important it is,

cannot be wasted,

yet always is.

Some sit and wish to turn back time.

Try a different way, choose a different choice.

Disappointed, something felt when I

think about my current situation

and how things could have been.

<u>Regret</u>

Full;

still not complete,

words never said,

people who'll never meet.

Goals;

became a distant thought,

couldn't accomplish,

and struggled a lot.

Stuck;

thinking about the past,

what change can be made,

things never really last.

Change;

always something new to regret,

trying not to lose sanity,

time, I don't know where it went.

Forget;

can't erase what's been done,

the struggle will remain,

if the heart keeps beating like a drum.

Feel;

it will continue to be real,

can't erase memories,

got to learn how to deal.

Cope;

can't change things,

or maybe make a change now,

learn lessons about what life brings.

Wisdom;

growing from a mistake,

create a life that's good,

it depends on choices you make.

Forward;

walk away from who you used to be,

is it too late,

for a new destiny?

Lead;

be different,

can the cycle be broken,

can the chains be lifted?

Remorse;

guilt and sorrow fill me up,

with wrong choices made,

like a half-empty cup.

End;

became too careless,

can't dwell on what should have been,

just become fearless.

Insecurity

I guess you didn't know something about me.

Let me clarify so you can step into my reality.

I guess I can be a little hard to read.

Could be because of my insecurity.

I wasn't always like this.

I would run around free and careless.

I could publicly speak with no stress.

An opinion couldn't affect the way I dress.

While I was trying to be innocent and play

I would be distracted by media that would display

how a person should look and what they should say.

This unexpected reality led to my dismay.

I became insecure inside.

Couldn't fit in so I would hide.

Their unrealistic image destroyed my pride,

which led to a short measurement in my stride.

Because I couldn't be tainted,

like the fake image they created.

Their true beauty is contaminated

by a face that has been covered and painted.

And my body is supposed to be perfect,

if not then they lose respect.

So I have to reshape or inject

to look like the image they expect.

Society, have you lost your mind?

You created insecurity when you lied.

With your technology you restructured mankind,

and natural beauty is now denied.

Insecurity would have never existed

if we all realized it's OK to be different

and know they created false images with their equipment.

Don't continue to be ignorant.

Insecurity can disappear

once we let go of that self-image fear.

Don't always believe what you see or hear.

Be natural, not insecure.

Beauty

Soft, glowing skin;

admiration.

Natural, pure, textured hair.

Beauty that's rare.

A graceful, rhythmic move;

every inch feels smooth.

Lips full of rose pedals,

beauty that's special.

Cheeks full and round;

voice of an angelic sound.

Beauty shines

through those hypnotizing eyes.

A unique, perfect face,

no mistakes.

A beauty cannot be compared;

an artwork shared.

A hand-crafted body

worth modeling.

Every eye can see

true beauty.

<u>Want</u>

A sexy glance from a stranger across the way

begins the passion of a sensual crave.

Every body part covered with clothes,

unfold…and discover my body like gold.

Moans and groans as our bodies sway.

Dripping fruit of ecstasy as pleasure is made.

Strokes of burning desire and lust,

tightening and stretching with every thrust.

Sweat slides with the friction

as you become my addiction.

I yearn for more as we move our waists.

My forbidden fruit is throbbing and wanting to taste.

I can't stop wanting until the strokes heal my pleasure pain,

aching for relief as you breathe over me where I lay,

and kiss me seductively as I fade

into a trance of a lovemaking parade.

Hold me, rub me, caress me within.

I'm high on what's forbidden;

these feelings that come from your physical form.

Be gentle while you perform.

Ease my craving with your tongue.

Touch me slowly with your love.

I see the orgasmic feelings in your eyes.

I hear the erotic sensation in your moaning cries.

Lie down while I taste your sweet cream,

then feel you inside me.

Feel my love with every motion I do,

I want you.

Keep It Real

I've listened to so many lies.

I have no more tears left to cry.

I'm sorry if I seem so cold.

I don't mean to come across so bold,

but I really don't want to play any games.

If you knew me you would feel the same.

My heart's been beat up so many times.

I'm surprised my love still survives.

But I won't let my guard down for you

unless your actions show me the truth.

You shouldn't try to sell me a dream

Because I really don't care about money.

What I need is a man to love me

and shield me from storms of the sea.

I'll be by my man's side through thick and thin.

I won't let anything come between me and him.

His burdens become mine.

Our lifestyles will align.

Even though old love didn't last

his presence erases my past.

So do you think you'll make me your wife?

Our marriage would be rife.

If you have doubts don't waste my time

since I'm not the definition of a dime.

Because I'm not like the average girl.

I don't fall into the stereotypical world.

So keep in mind that I am real,

and tell my how you really feel.

Dance

You see me alone,

pull me off my seat.

Move to the rhythm

of the passionate beat.

Hold me close

as my body gets weak.

Support my back

while you direct my feet.

Gaze into my eyes

as we feel the love heat.

Sway side to side,

now two lovers meet.

Our love is strong

and no one can defeat.

The bond we've created

have made enemies retreat.

Dance with only me

because no other can ever compete.

<u>Vows</u>

When I first met you I didn't know

that God was molding our love to grow

and we were preparing for each other all those years ago.

You are the definition of a man,

you make me want to be a better woman,

and I will stand by you no matter what may happen.

Your intelligence is inspiring,

your ambition is aspiring,

because of you my heart can't stop smiling.

Your smile and eyes amaze me,

everything about you is amazing.

You are my Prince Charming.

You are a blessing that came unexpectedly,

God designed you perfectly

to love me attentively.

I promise to love you unconditionally,

because our bond is un-destructible,

because our love is un-measurable, because I cherish you so.

I promise to take care of you when you are down,

to love you when no one else is around,

to support you when you've fallen to the ground.

I promise to bring happiness to our life,

to fix any conflict or strife,

to be the definition of a wife.

I commit to love you,

to support you no matter what we go through,

and cheerlead you on with your dreams to pursue.

Our love was designed in God's plan;

God's angels celebrated when our love began;

I know you are meant to be my husband.

Dear Child

Peace, I breath in

as I gaze upon your precious face.

I'm hypnotized at the perfection

of what love can create.

You calm me

and fill my soul with happiness.

The very thought of my baby

reminds me that I am blessed.

Your gentleness

relaxes my every mood.

I am cured by your kiss;

with your presence I am consumed.

Innocent child given to this earth,

inside me you grew

as I anticipated your birth

and protected you in my womb.

Grow to be great;

be better than me.

Conquer your own fate

and be the model of a human being.

I will protect you from all evil.

I will provide wisdom others cannot comprehend.

You will be aware of what's lethal

and not let anything reprogram your head.

My child, I will build you strong.

You will succeed with little struggle,

and know what is right from wrong

because I am your mother.

<u>Sunlight</u>

Midday sunlight,

with its warmth,

touches the flower

with a splash of paint.

Creating life's work of art.

The masterpiece is vivid in color.

This sight, no photo can ever imitate

these natural light settings.

Once the glorious sunrays

depart

from the flower,

the beauty emerges as pleasant,

yet not as

powerful.

<u>Good-Bye Dad</u>

Dad, how would it have been

if you were here.

If you had seen me become a woman.

I hold on to you through memories,

the short moments.

I'll introduce you to your grandbabies

through your portraits.

The day I said good-bye

I wish you would have never left.

I was too young to know why

and didn't know what to expect.

Did you miss us when you were gone?

Were you lonely?

Did you know it would be this long?

Did you always think of me?

I needed guidance from you,

you should have stayed.

Did you know

we would struggle from mistakes you made?

I needed you when I was in college;

motivating me to study

and continue to gain knowledge

and supporting me.

I needed you to call me princess,

hold my hand while walking down the aisle,

complimenting my dress,

and holding my first child.

I needed a father to go to

when the stress of life was too much,

and you would always know what to do

and calm me while we ate our favorite lunch.

I wonder if things would be different

or if I would be the same.

Guess I'll never know now since you went,

but I'll still pass on your name.

Although I miss our patty-cake sessions

after a long day at school.

And all your valuable lessons

and the jokes you thought were cool.

Come visit me if you can,

even for just a short time.

If you can't, I understand;

you'll always be in my mind.

My Perception

Life could be so amazing

if you look at it through heaven's eyes.

Experiences can become discouraging

and fill your heart with worries.

The past can make you or break you,

and people can become threatening.

If you hold on to a distance

you'll never find the ending.

It's so hard to keep your head up when

everything around you is broken.

There's no direction for you to go;

every path you take becomes a closed door.

If you struggle and not achieve anything,

was it worth all the suffering.

It's better to look at life differently

to make it through the hard things.

Although we focus on what could have been

we still survive in the life we are in.

I'm just sharing the visions in my heart

whether you hear me or not.

<u>See</u>

Help the children see,

let their voices come from within.

Rescue them from their sin.

Take away the name of fear.

Help them find a path that's clear.

Bravery,

cleanse their mind of weakness.

Courage,

stand and pull them to no limits.

Creativity

is what they need.

Help them to be positive in theory.

Believe,

the only way they will achieve.

Mind, brain, thinking.

Help them to see.

Think

You think you see

images disguised as a dream.

You think you know

lectures of history that are untold.

Hidden from all who choose to believe.

Reality is what they deceive.

Yet continue your education in the dark.

Keep learning from end to start.

Go down a guided path of the dead end.

Get lost and be found by them.

Stay a part of the assembly line.

Follow the rules that keep you blind.

Knowledge is yours to discover.

Without truth you continue to suffer.

You feel you have access to it all,

then why do you continue to fall?

It's a maze with no way out.

A design without room for doubt.

How do you find knowledge with no direction?

Who can teach it when the rules are deception?

How will we leave this jail?

When do we realize when we fail?

I see with eyes deceived by visions.

My personality is molded by false decisions.

My intuition was beaten by a social system.

My true voice, once heard, yet they never listen.

I am led by what I feel.

I want to see what is real.

Social Conspiracy

Nowadays, in order to see a familiar face,

I got to open a web page.

What's happening to our human race,

our society ain't the same.

This generation looks at a screen

to communicate with loved ones they haven't seen.

When did we get programmed to

technology that got us stuck like glue.

Instead of looking up to smile

at the person across the table,

we look down at the phone for a while

until the battery dies and we are unable.

The human touch became hard to come by,

but a swipe is made easy.

For human contact I have to go outside

and hope that they will look up at me.

It's crazy how I can get more conversation via phone

and rely on technology to reach out to a friend.

It's like we've become more social alone.

When did social gatherings end?

What happened to days when kids played outside,

while adults were bragging?

Kids ran around to hide,

I guess we got too busy video chatting.

<u>Through His Eyes</u>

Waking up to arguments and fights,

abuse and drug use,

things just never get right.

See the pain through my eyes.

Did you ever feel like your mom and dad didn't love you,

but you're too young,

no one will think what you say is true.

So you have to live with the abuse.

All you know is beatings,

all you seen is anger and hitting,

all you hear is crying and screaming,

all you feel is your wounds bleeding.

The only outlet you get is Sunday school teaching.

You stare at the teacher and wonder if she can see

the misery that you endured all week.

Can she see why you don't smile?

Does she know the truth when everyone is in denial?

Can she make you feel loved for a little while?

They say he's shy and that's why he doesn't talk.

The real reason is they break his legs to the point that he can't walk.

This boy doesn't know what love is.

This boy doesn't know what a hug is.

This boy doesn't know how to play outside

because he's isolated and only knows how to hide.

You'll never see his happiness

because he grew up not learning this.

How come nobody saves him?

Why do they stay quiet and keep it within?

Why don't they get help and

get him out?

Why do they let the abuse continue?

Why do they feel there's nothing they can do?

This boy had the world of opportunity

and he died at only three.

Be the voice for the children who can't speak.

Be strong when they are weak.

Protect God's children from the devil's hand.

Be the guidance to lead them to the promised land.

This boy lived in a system that failed him.

Be the one who prevents the children

from being a victim.

Dark Man

He enters the café,

exhausted and sweaty from the hot sun.

Everyone stops and stares,

as he paces his breath from his run.

The judging eyes pierce his,

while he gathers his composure to more formal.

He's afraid to gaze back,

because he senses he is not normal.

Is it because of his black skin,

he wonders while avoiding eye contact.

Is it the clothes he's wearing,

or the old dirty backpack?

He sits down on a chair,

others around get up and leave.

He looks down and wonders why,

is he some type of enemy.

Middle-aged black man,

who used to have hopes and dreams.

Grew up in a cruel world,

and shortly realized reality.

Opportunities were never easy,

and did not come to him.

He tried to make it,

yet doors were never opened.

Wherever he goes they stop and look,

he causes fear in others.

Based on the way society tainted,

the image of his skin colors.

Dark-skinned man you are strong,

black man from Africa be proud.

Don't let other colors destroy your pride,

keep your head up from facing the ground.

<u>The Melanin Print</u>

To hate me is to hate the very image of the creator,

for I am not lighter

but the same color as the ground,

and my bloodline is all around.

My ancestors, the Moors,

who've traveled the world,

created most things that we now know.

So why is my color hated so?

Go to the ancient worlds and you will see

the roots of my African history.

The most resourceful continent

has been oppressed to be one of the poorest on this planet.

Don't deny my intelligence because of my dark hue,

don't belittle me because I do not resemble you.

You cannot hide the truth for long;

knowledge is power and my people will catch on.

Through the harsh events of this earth

my dominant genes will show you my worth.

We will connect to our true spirituality

and be more powerful than the average human being.

Karma, as you will see, has taken its course.

My connection to the universe

can be found in my melanin;

the pigment that makes my skin the hue of my dark complexion.

You cannot deny my African heritage,

because across the world you'll find African footprints.

African people, be proud of your race.

Don't let anyone try to erase

the truth of our African world;

the truth of who is our Lord.

Don't be deceived by what you are led to believe.

Remember the oldest bones ever found was African Lucy.

<u>Step</u>

Stepped into shoes;

I never thought I would

do the things I put my mind to.

Now I know what I'm capable of,

yet the unfortunate reality

is I won't get very far in this society.

See, even though I'm a mixed within,

they only can see my skin

and care less about the story I tell them.

They know I have goals,

so they set limits for me,

they are unaware I serve a higher being.

They've made it difficult for certain people;

see, they can try to break me with their rule,

but I'll keep trying since I know what's true.

They might think they'll stop me,

they can always try;

though I won't be another statistic in their mind.

I've stepped over the walls and the obstacles;

"can't" is not in my vocabulary,

for I know the power I have internally.

Knowledge of the truth fuels my motivation;

I've steadily analyzed choices to make.

While they sleep, I stay awake

thinking of the next move.

I got to step out of the social distraction

and remember that change takes action.

Step out of place,

step out of the dark cave,

and face obstacles headed my way.

They won't deny me from what is mine;

my moral values will not be ignored.

I know who is my Lord.

<u>Closing the Chapter</u>

Looking back in the past

of a lifetime of memories

can create mixed emotions

when thinking of what used to be.

Now that life is still going

and time is still short,

I am satisfied with the stories

in my book of life that I wrote.

We think things happen for a reason

and environments shape personalities,

you create the path you walk on

and choose to find your destiny.

Yet, I think you build your world

with the tool of your brain,

and you choose to be happy

or dwell on your pain.

Thinking of the past will keep you stuck

and prevent you from learning from your mistakes,

if you choose to live in misery

in which a grudge creates.

Let it go, and move on,

for you can't change what's been done,

so live for the present memories

and create new ones.

Close the chapter of an old story

so you can open a new page,

and use your new wisdom

to make your life change.

You can't control people

or events that will come to be,

yet you can control your actions

and how you handle what you're feeling.

If you can't forget about the past

then create something new

and design a better future past

because now your story is created by you.

ABOUT THE AUTHOR

Maha Griffin is a self-taught writer with a natural talent of finding ways to express herself through the art of poetry. She grew up in the urban area of central San Diego, where she learned the hardships of poverty. Maha's mother raised her, along with her three brothers, as a single parent. Her father left her at the age of nine and passed away when Maha was seventeen.

A poet who began writing at the age of ten, Maha submitted her early work during her teen years to Poetry.com and received two editor's choice awards in 2003 and 2008. Her writing style was influenced by rap music, which motivated her to write urban poetry. In 2013 she graduated from San Diego State University with a bachelor of science degree in child development and eventually returned to the university to complete her master of social work.

Maha currently works as an adoption social worker. *Poetry of the Heart: A Journey through Emotions* is her first book of poetry.